Exploring Music

Strings

Alyn Shipton

RAINTREE
STECK-VAUGHN
PUBLISHERS
The Steck-Vaughn Company

Austin, Texas

3588001

Titles in the Series
Brass
Keyboards and Electronic Music
Percussion
Singing
Strings
Woodwinds

Edited by Pauline Tait and Mary Sullivan
Consultant: Skipp Tullen
Picture research by Suzanne Williams
Designed by Julian Holland
Illustrator: Terry Hadler
Electronic Production: Scott Melcer

Picture acknowledgments

Raintree Steck-Vaughn Publishers would like to thank Edgarley Hall School music department, especially Mr. Brian Armfield, for assistance with commissioned photography; and David Titchener for supplying the photographs.

The author and publishers wish to thank the following photographic sources: The Bridgeman Art Library, Michelangelo Caravaggio (1573-1610) *A Young Man Playing the Lute*, The Hermitage, St. Petersburg, p4; E. T. Archive: p8 (top), p14; Giraudon: Jean-Marc Nattier (1685-1766) *Madame Henriette jouant de la basse de viole* Chateau de Versailles p9; Michael Holford: p8 (bottom), p16, p28; Performing Arts Library/Clive Barda: p15, p17, p29 (top); Redferns: title page/Sean Hudson, p21, p27 (top); Courtesy of Sotheby's, London: p27 (bottom); © Eileen Polk/LGI: p23; © Steve Jennings/LGI: p25; Zefa: p29 (bottom right).

Cover credits
(harp) Performing Arts Library/Clive Barda; (flamenco style guitar) © Eileen Polk/LGI; (children with violins) Redferns/Odile Noel.

Library of Congress Cataloging-in-Publication Data

Shipton, Alyn.
    Strings / Alyn Shipton.
       p.   cm. — (Exploring music)
    Includes index.
    Summary: An introduction to the string family of intruments, such as the violin, viola, cello, harp, guitar and their relatives.
      ISBN 0-8114-2320-4
      1. Stringed instruments — Juvenile literature.   [1. Stringed instruments.]
    I. Title.   II. Series: Shipton, Alyn. Exploring music.
    ML460.S55   1994
    787'.19—dc20   93-15278
                                              CIP
                                         AC MN

Printed and bound in the United States
1 2 3 4 5 6 7 8 9 0 VHP 99 98 97 96 95 94 93

Contents

How String Instruments Work

Guitar and lute players developed the **plectrum** when they needed a more powerful way to strum chords. The plectrum, sometimes called a pick, is a triangle of horn, shell, or plastic that is held in the hand and drawn up or down across the strings. On the right is a "ring" plectrum, which fits around the index finger of the right hand and is used like an artificial fingernail.

All string instruments have one thing in common. The vibration of their strings produces their sound. The kind of sound each makes depends on how its strings are made to vibrate. The sizes of the strings themselves also affect the sound.

Some instruments, like the guitar, the banjo, and the lute, have strings that are plucked. Other instruments, like the violin, are played with a special bow.

A lute player painted by Caravaggio in the late 16th century

PLUCKED INSTRUMENTS

Guitars and lutes are played by plucking the strings. A player can "strum" chords by sounding several strings at once with the tips of the fingers of the right hand. It is also possible to use the fingertips or nails to pick out a series of individual melody notes. Players have developed **finger-picking** by putting these two techniques together. They play a melody and pluck chords at the same time. Finger-picking is popular in blues and country and western music, although it came from traditional and classical Spanish guitar music.

Sound

Anything that vibrates makes a sound. When the vibrations pass through the air to our ears, we hear the sound. This is because as something vibrates, it pushes or pulls the air nearby and sets up sound waves that travel through the air.

Using an electronic instrument called an oscilloscope we can make pictures of sound waves on a televisionlike screen. These show us that sound waves come in a variety of shapes and sizes. Some are broad, slow waves, others are fast and agitated. This is because the vibrations—the sounds—that cause the waves are all different themselves. Our ears tell sounds from one another by identifying three things:

volume: how loud the sound is;

pitch: how high or low it is; and

tone: the type or quality of the sound

BOWED INSTRUMENTS

Another group of string instruments, the violin family especially, is designed to be played with the bow. The bow is made with horsehair roughened with resin, which is dragged across the strings. This makes them sound a continuous note, instead of the short, sharp sounds produced by finger-picking or plectrum strumming. Ancient instruments like the viol used the bow as well. When bowed instruments are plucked, they produce an effect called **pizzicato** that contrasts with the smooth sound of the bow.

A violinist draws the bow across the strings of her instrument. The inset shows how the roughened hairs make the string vibrate.

The Parts of a String Instrument

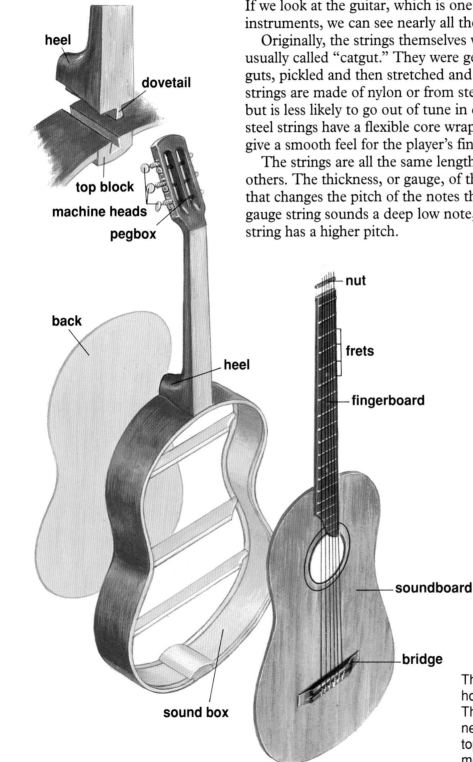

heel

dovetail

top block

machine heads

pegbox

back

heel

nut

frets

fingerboard

sound box

soundboard

bridge

If we look at the guitar, which is one of the most common string instruments, we can see nearly all the features of the string family.

Originally, the strings themselves were made from animal gut, usually called "catgut." They were generally made from lambs' guts, pickled and then stretched and polished. Today, most guitar strings are made of nylon or from steel. Nylon lasts as long as gut but is less likely to go out of tune in damp or hot weather. Some steel strings have a flexible core wrapped with a flat steel tape, to give a smooth feel for the player's fingers.

The strings are all the same length, but some are thicker than others. The thickness, or gauge, of the strings is one of the factors that changes the pitch of the notes they produce. A thick, heavy gauge string sounds a deep low note, while a thinner, light gauge string has a higher pitch.

The diagram on the left shows how a Spanish guitar is made. There are two ways of joining the neck to the body of the guitar. The top diagram shows the "dovetail" method.

SOUND BOX

The body of the guitar is called its **sound box**. The vibrations of the strings pass through the **bridge** onto the **soundboard**, and this **resonates**, amplifying, or increasing, the sound through the round sound hole. The soundboard, or belly, of the guitar is flat, and it has a simple circular sound hole, but in some other string instruments the belly is curved, and the sound holes can vary in shape. The strings are stretched from the **nut** at the top of the fingerboard to the bridge.

TUNING

At the top of the **fingerboard** is the **pegbox**. The earliest guitars just had a flat piece of wood here, with six **tuning** pegs wedged through it. Today, guitars have an open pegbox with little gears called **machine heads** to adjust the **tension** of the strings. The tighter a string is, the higher the note it produces. Most string instruments have tuning pegs or machine heads to tune the strings.

CHANGING THE NOTES

The main way string instruments change the note they play is by altering the length of string that is free to vibrate and make a sound. The shorter the string, the higher the note it produces. The longer the string, the lower the note it plays. The fingerboard of the guitar has several metal bars set across it. These are called **frets**, and the player uses them to change the note made by each string. If a player puts a finger just in front of the fret and presses down, the length of the string that can vibrate freely is shortened, and so the pitch of the note is raised. Some instruments, like the violin family, do not have frets, and it is the player's left hand fingers alone that alter the length of vibrating strings.

The guitar is designed so the player can change the notes of all six strings at once. Look at the illustration to see how this can be done. By plucking or strumming all the strings together, the player produces **chords**. Strumming chords one after the other is a good way to play with or **accompany** a singer.

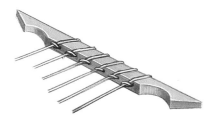

The bridge of the guitar
The lower ends of the strings are loops. They are threaded through holes in the bridge and fastened.

A guitarist holding down a chord with the left hand and strumming with the right hand.

Early Instruments

The angel in this section from an Italian painting is playing a rebec.

THE REBEC

The rebec was in use in Europe as early as the 10th century. The rebec is a simple bowed instrument with a pear-shaped body that runs smoothly into the fingerboard. Its ancestor was the Arab *rabab*. By the Middle Ages, the rebec was usually played with a simple arched bow, and held either on the lap (like a baby cello) or at chest height. It was a favorite instrument of professional minstrels who played at the courts of European kings and queens. Many paintings from the 13th to the 16th century show rebecs being played by angels or courtiers. Some instruments were elaborately carved.

THE KIT

The kit was a tiny rebec and later became more like a tiny violin, with a very thin body but an almost full-sized fingerboard. In France it was called the *poche*, or "pocket," because dancing masters kept the instrument in a special leather pouch. In England it was also used by dancing masters to accompany their pupils, but it was nicknamed "kit" or "kitten" to the violin.

The two musicians on the left of this picture, from a 13th-century illuminated manuscript, are holding spade-shaped fiddles.

THE FIDDLE

The fiddle was common in Europe in the Middle Ages. It was often oval or spade-shaped, with a flat belly and back, and was quite different from the rebec and the viol. The sound holes of the fiddle were C-shaped, and, as the sides started to be curved inward to help the player use the bow more easily, the instrument became more like the modern violin. Some traditional fiddles are still in use today. The *mazanki* is a small folk fiddle from Poland, while the *träskofiol* or "clog-fiddle" from Sweden is carved out of a wooden shoe. Perhaps the best-known folk fiddle is the Hardanger fiddle from western Norway, which is often beautifully decorated and has additional "sympathetic" strings that sound when the main strings are bowed.

THE VIOL

From the 1400s to the 1700s, the most popular bowed instrument was the viol. The viol was played on the lap (or for larger members of the family, held between the player's knees). It looked like the modern cello but was made in several sizes. Viols had frets, made of gut, and they usually had six strings. Much music was written for groups, or **consorts**, of viols. As time went on their thin, reedy, delicate sound became less popular than the brighter, louder violin family.

Listening Guide

Many of the early string instruments that vanished from use hundreds of years ago have been rediscovered and are being played again. They hold a special interest for both player and listener because of their sound. Viols and rebecs can be heard on recordings by the Early Music Consort and the Academy of Ancient Music.

An 18th-century French painting of a viola da gamba lesson. This is one of the largest members of the viol family.

The Violin and Viola

Even today, in some parts of the United States, and in some European folk music, the violin is still held and played somewhat like a rebec, resting on the chest. For over two hundred years, most classical players have held the violin and its larger sibling, the viola, under their chins. In the mid-1700s, Leopold Mozart, father of the famous composer, wrote a book, or "treatise," on how to play the violin. By his time, the player supported the instrument entirely with the chin, leaving the left hand to move freely on the fingerboard and alter the notes.

The violins made in the 18th century were of the type still in use today. Antonio Stradivari (1644–1737) was the greatest of all violin builders. His instruments and those of other great makers like Amati and Guarnieri are used by the world's greatest soloists, and today are worth hundreds of thousands of dollars each.

This young violinist is holding her violin and bow in the modern playing position.

THE VIOLA

The viola has a deeper sound than the violin and is pitched lower. Wolfgang Amadeus Mozart wrote his *Sinfonia Concertante* of 1779 for both violin and viola as solo instruments. The contrasts between the two instruments can be clearly heard in this work. Like his father, Mozart played both instruments, and he knew exactly how to get the best out of them. Few solo compositions have been written for the viola, although it has been a favorite of English composers, including William Walton, who wrote a concerto for it.

This young person is playing the viola, which is larger than the violin shown opposite.

THE NECK AND SCROLL

The pegbox of the violin and viola is contained in the carved **scroll**. The four strings correspond to the tuning pegs. Those closest to the tip of the scroll control the middle strings, and those closer to the body of the instrument control the outer ones. The strings run over the nut and across the smooth ebony fingerboard, which is curved into a gently arched shape. The player's left-hand fingers **stop** the strings, and change the notes, using a series of special places or "positions," each at a particular point on the instrument.

Close-up detail of a violin showing the neck and scroll.

11

THE BRIDGE AND BODY

The belly of both instruments is curved and has two *f*-shaped sound holes. Running down the inside of the belly is a bar called the bass-bar. Standing between the front and the back of each instrument is the soundpost. Between the sound holes is the bridge, carved of light wood, and curved in a similar shape, or profile, to the fingerboard. The bridge carries the strings and is used to space them evenly and control their height. By careful bow control, the player can sound two strings at a time, playing simple chords, or keeping two independent melodies going together. This technique is called "double stopping."

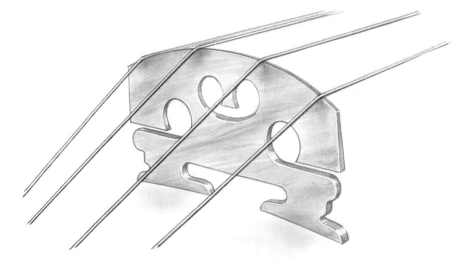

The wooden bridge of the violin has sections cut away for decoration and to improve the sound.

THE TAILPIECE AND CHINREST

At the far end from the scroll, the strings are attached to the tailpiece. Often they are joined to little levers called adjusters that give a fine degree of tuning that is hard to achieve with just the pegs. The chin rest, partially covering the tailpiece, is designed to make the instruments easy and comfortable to hold for both solo and orchestral players.

The chin rest is a shaped piece of ebony, ivory, or plastic attached to the violin with a metal clip. It helps the violinist grip the instrument between the chin and shoulder.

THE BOW

Early bows for rebecs, viols, and fiddles had a convex shape, curved like the outside of a circle, or like an archer's bow. By the late 18th century, the modern bow had developed. Its horsehair was secured into the bow at the far ("point") end and attached to an adjustable block called a **frog** at the end held by the player. The bow's shape had changed, dipping toward the strings in the middle. The frog was operated by a screw mechanism. The hair needed to be tight for playing but loosened when not in use, since changes in temperature could cause it to contract and snap. The bow, which is larger for the viola, is held in the player's right hand, just above the frog.

When violinists pluck the strings, in the technique called pizzicato, they hold the bow in their lower fingers and pluck with the forefinger.

Violin Playing

Many great violinists started to learn the instrument when they were very young. Violin makers have crafted half- and three-quarter-sized instruments that are so small children can reach to finger the strings properly with the left hand.

It can take a few months before a young player can control the **fingering** and the bow well enough to get a good sound, but with regular practice he or she can then progress quickly. A popular way of learning to play is the Japanese Suzuki method, in which classes of very young children learn to play together.

The orchestra leader is the first violin player, who sits at the front of the violin section.

Listening Guide

For four hundred years, the violin and its family have been the most important instruments of the orchestra. The violin can be used in all styles of music. Great concerti have been written for the violin by Beethoven and Mendelssohn, as well as many other composers, including the great violinists Paganini (1782–1840) and Fritz Kreisler (1875–1962) who wrote very different pieces. Recordings of violin music have been made by Kyung-Wha Chung, Yehudi Menuhin, Itzhak Perlman, and Pinchas Zuckerman.

As well as creating very popular classical recordings, Nigel Kennedy has played jazz on the violin, following in the great tradition of such players as Stephane Grappelli and Joe Venuti. Blues player "Gatemouth" Brown plays the instrument and so does folk-rock star Dave Swarbrick.

The Cello

If we think of the violin as a **soprano** singer, and the viola as an **alto**, the **tenor** voice of the violin family belongs to the cello. It is an instrument of extraordinary range and flexibility, called in full the violoncello. At first glance, it looks somewhat like the tenor viol (or *viola da gamba*), but it is different in many other ways. Originally, like the viol, it was held between the player's knees, but around the beginning of the 18th century a metal spike was added to support its weight. The viol had frets, but like the violin, the cello has a smooth fingerboard. The viol had six strings, the cello has only four.

The cello was developed during the 16th and 17th centuries, and the modern instrument follows the designs of Antonio Stradivari. Between 1707 and 1710, Stradivari built over 20 cellos that put his ideas into practice. These have been the model for most cello builders for nearly two hundred years.

One of the first composers to realize the potential of the cello was J.S. Bach, who wrote a series of long solos called "suites" for unaccompanied cello. The instrument's lowest C string is an **octave** below the viola, yet players can obtain notes well into the range of the violin by "stopping strings high up the fingerboard near the bridge. If you look at a player's hand, the left thumb is tucked behind the neck when fingering near the scroll. As the hand moves toward the bridge, the thumb moves to the front of the fingerboard and is used as a kind of pivot. The players call these positions "thumb positions." Bach's solo suites use the instrument's full range.

Johann Sebastian Bach (1685–1750) who composed six cello suites, was one of a large family of composers. Over a dozen of his children, grandchildren, and cousins wrote music.

Cello Playing

Even though there are half-sized cellos for young children to use, most cellists begin when they are big enough to play the full-sized instrument, at around the age of eleven. Like all the other string instruments, playing the cello involves control of both hands doing different things as the left hand changes the notes and the right hand operates the bow. Once a player has mastered this, swift progress can be made, and there is a huge variety of solo music, chamber music, and orchestral music to play. To get started, it is a good idea to borrow a cello from a school or orchestra. Then you can develop to a level where you can choose an instrument that suits your playing. Cello strings are expensive to replace, bows need re-hairing occasionally, and the varnish on the instrument needs to be cared for.

If you compare the hand positions used by the cellist with those of the violinist or viola player, you will see they are very different. Even the bow is held differently. As the instrument itself has developed, with more sophisticated endpins (or spikes), and different designs of bridge and tailpiece, players have learned to get more control over the instrument.

Listening Guide

Most of the great cellists of this century have made many recordings. Pablo Casals (1876–1973) recorded the Bach suites and the Dvořák concerto in the 1930s, and his recordings are still widely listened to. Other great players, including Paul Tortelier (on the left), Jacqueline de Pré, and Mstislav Rostropovich have recorded works including the concertos by Elgar and Saint-Saëns, and the sonatas by Beethoven and Brahms. Among the best younger players to record are Yo Yo Ma and Julian Lloyd Webber.

Relatives of the Cello

An instrument similar to the cello in range and sound, but in reality a kind of bowed guitar, was the *arpeggione*. This was invented around 1823 by J.G. Stauffer of Vienna. The arpeggione had 24 frets, six strings, and a smooth-sided, guitarlike shape. It was not popular, and the fine sonata written for it by Shubert is now usually played on the cello.

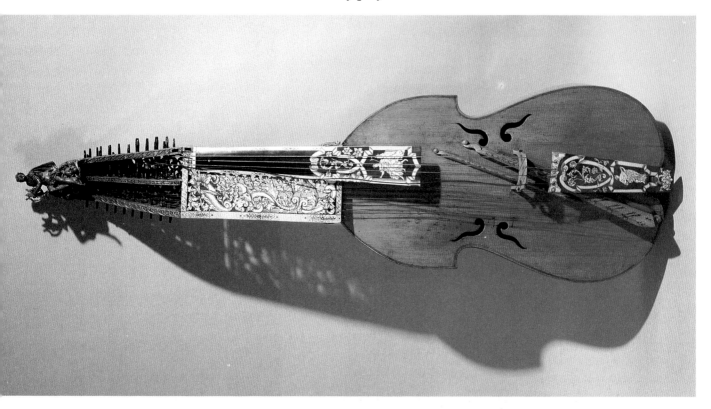

A German baryton that was made around 1720

The *baryton* is an earlier and much more extraordinary instrument. It looks like a cross between a cello, a bass viol, and a large lute called a *theorbo*. As well as a set of bowed strings the baryton has additional strings that either resonate on their own ("sympathetic strings"), or which are designed to be plucked by the player's left thumb. Very little music would have survived for this difficult, faddish instrument had not Prince Nikolaus of Esterhazy become interested in it in 1765. Prince Nikolaus loved music and employed a private orchestra and several composers. His main composer was Joseph Haydn. The prince asked Haydn to write large amounts of new chamber music for him to play on the baryton. Haydn and his fellow court composers produced dozens of pieces over the next few years. Haydn himself learned the instrument in secret, only to be scolded by the prince for becoming too skillful!

In many countries of the world, there are folk instruments related to the cello. One of the more unusual is the *gardon*, which is used by gypsy musicians in Hungary and Transylvania. It has three and sometimes four strings. The player either hits the strings with a stick or slaps them against the fingerboard, producing a rhythmic accompaniment to other gypsy instruments, such as the violin.

THE STRING QUARTET

The combination of two violins, viola, and cello is known as the string **quartet**, and many composers have been fascinated by the possibilities of writing for this set of string voices. Joseph Haydn wrote nearly 70 string quartets between about 1760 and 1803. Mozart, Beethoven, and Shubert all wrote for this group of instruments as well. Many 20th-century composers have written string quartets. Roger Sessions, Darius Milhaud, and Ernst Bloch wrote several for the Griller String Quartet at Berkeley, California. They introduced a number of new pieces to the public over a period of 13 years.

The Allegri String Quartet

The Double Bass

The biggest of the bowed string instruments is the double bass. In shape, basses often resemble viols, as they tend to have sloping "shoulders," and sometimes a flat back with a sharp angle just below the neck. Other basses are built to look much more like large violins. The double bass has a smooth, fretless fingerboard and, as with the cello, the use of the high "thumb positions" gives it a huge range.

Basses are found in all symphony orchestras. They are used in **chamber** groups and sometimes as **solo** instruments. Over 200 concerti have been written for the bass. In the early 1900s, the bass was found in the small orchestras that played **ragtime** in America. From there, it found its way into **jazz**. It has been used by country and western and traditional folk music groups. During the 1950s, a primitive bass was often made from a washtub and broom handle with a single string.

A modern double bass
This picture clearly shows the sloping "shoulders" where the neck joins the body.

THE SCROLL AND PEGBOX

Look closely at the picture of the tuning mechanism of the bass. There is a gear wheel on the end of each tuning peg, operated by gears on the keys. Originally, basses had large pegs that looked like those of a cello, but these slipped out of tune easily, and fine adjustments were hard to make. The other diagram shows the **extension** fitted to some basses that runs above the scroll and extends the low E string down four notes to a C. Levers operated by the player's left hand stop the string beyond the end of the fingerboard. Normally the strings of a bass are tuned (from the bottom) E-A-D-G. The extension means players can use their normal fingering positions but have four extra notes available (C-C♯-D-D♯). Composers often write music that includes these low notes for the bass, and so extensions are common. Some players prefer a five-string instrument. This involves learning a whole new set of fingering since all the strings are tuned differently.

Left: a close-up of the extension that gives the bass a bottom note of C. The four levers on the right operate keys that "stop" the string.

Right: the tuning mechanism of the bass with the strings removed to show the pegs that are worked by the gear wheel outside.

THE BOW

In many orchestras, the bows used by the bassist look like larger versions of cello bows. They are a little thicker and have a wider band of hair in order to play the big, heavy strings more effectively. This kind of bow is called the "French bow." Often, you will see another kind of bow with a much larger frog, that is held from underneath. This is a "German" bow and is very close to the old styles of bow used for viols and rebecs. Both styles of bow are in common use in today's orchestras and chamber groups.

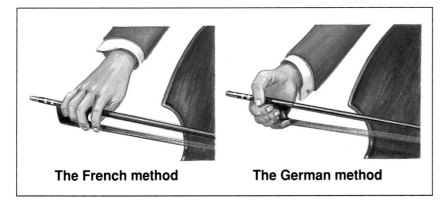

The French method   **The German method**

BOWING AND PIZZICATO

In most forms of classical music the bass is played with the bow. Some composers ask for the bass to be plucked. Just like the violin, the musical term for this is pizzicato. Instead of the drawn-out sound of notes that last as long as the bow is moving, pizzicato playing produces short, abrupt sounds. In popular music and jazz, the bass is plucked almost all the time, and it is bowed only occasionally.

GREAT BASSISTS

Although many composers have written for the bass, not much of this work is well known. Most people think of Saint-Saëns's slow, ponderous bass solo "The Elephant" from his *Carnival of the Animals* as typical bass music. Two players who tried to change things are Serge Koussevitzky, who was a fine bassist before becoming a conductor, and Gary Karr. Koussevitzky wrote pieces for the bass himself, while Karr has commissioned many composers to write for him.

This player is demonstrating pizzicato, where the bass strings are plucked with the fingers of the right hand.

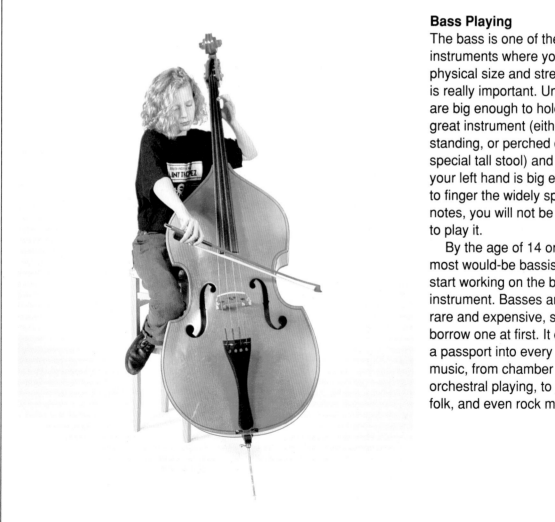

Bass Playing

The bass is one of the few instruments where your physical size and strength is really important. Until you are big enough to hold this great instrument (either standing, or perched on a special tall stool) and until your left hand is big enough to finger the widely spaced notes, you will not be able to play it.

By the age of 14 or so, most would-be bassists can start working on the big instrument. Basses are fairly rare and expensive, so try to borrow one at first. It can be a passport into every kind of music, from chamber and orchestral playing, to jazz, folk, and even rock music.

THE PICCOLO BASS

This small version of the bass, which sounds an octave higher, was developed in the United States during the 1960s by jazz players Ray Brown and Ron Carter. It sounds like a pizzicato cello but was developed for bassists to play fast plucked solos in a high range.

OTHER BASSES

In the classical period, the *violone* was still in use. This was a very large viol, with frets and six strings. It was gradually replaced by the double bass.

In this century, instrument builders tried to make smaller versions of the large double bass, using electronics to amplify its sound. The body has been made thinner and smaller, but the fingerboard has remained the same. German bassist Eberhard Weber has used an electric "stick" bass since 1972.

Listening Guide
To hear the classical bass at its best, listen to records by Gary Karr. Jazz players who have made recordings on the bass include Charles Mingus, Ray Brown, Milt Hinton, and Oscar Pettiford. Some of the most unusual records ever made are the duets by bassist Jimmy Blanton and the pianist Duke Ellington including "Pitter Panther Patter." Ray Brown, shown here, made new recordings of these duets. Recordings of bassist Slam Stewart are noteworthy, too.

The Guitar

A traditional Spanish guitar

At the beginning of this book we looked at how the guitar is typical of many string instruments. The modern guitar has six strings, a neck with 19 frets, and many different shapes of sound box. The traditional Spanish guitar is the most widely used. As one of the most popular instruments in the world today, the guitar has developed into a bewildering number of shapes and types. It is used in almost every style of music, and instrument builders have invented new kinds of guitars for the particular needs of each style. Many of the guitars in use today are "electric guitars" designed to be played through an amplifier. First, we should look at the Spanish guitar.

THE SPANISH GUITAR

The present-day Spanish guitar dates from the early 1800s. Before this, guitars were smaller, some having only four strings, with a wide variety of tuning systems. The modern instrument has the familiar figure-eight sound box, a round sound hole, nylon strings, and machine head tuning **keys**. For some styles of music, metal strings are used, which produce a louder, harsher sound.

The strings of a guitar are called "courses." This dates from the time when more than one string would be tuned to the same note. Today's 12-string guitar has the strings tuned in pairs—in other words, it has six courses of two strings each.

The Spanish guitar is usually played sitting down, supported on the left thigh, as shown in this picture.

A Spanish guitar played in typical flamenco style

OTHER ACOUSTIC GUITARS

Most classical guitar music is written for the Spanish guitar. This is the instrument used in Spanish and French flamenco gypsy music, as well as in music from many parts of South and Central America. In the United States, a Czech guitar maker named John Doperya invented a new kind of guitar. Part of the sound box was made of metal. In the 1920s, his "National" company made these instruments, which were called "dobro" guitars. Their heavy, metallic sound became very popular with blues singers.

At about the same time an Italian designer, Mario Maccaferri, invented a kind of guitar that became very popular with European jazz and gypsy musicians, such as Django Reinhardt. Maccaferri's design had a second wooden sound box inside the main body of the guitar, which gave his metal-string instruments great volume and strength. These instruments had a D-shaped sound hole and often had a corner of the sound box cut away, so the player's left hand could play chords at the very top of the fingerboard.

The Electric Guitar

During the 1920s and 1930s, the first attempts were made to produce electrically amplified guitars. Players wanted to be heard in groups that contained loud trumpets, saxophones, and drums, all of which drowned out the quiet **acoustic guitar**. The Gibson and Rickenbacker companies made ordinary guitars with magnetic **pickups**. A pickup converts the sound made by the strings into electric pulses. These signals are converted back into much louder sounds by an amplifier. Today, many give credit to Les Paul for having invented the electric guitar.

Gradually, as makers realized that electric guitars did not need to be built with the same type of sound box as acoustic instruments, the bodies of electric guitars changed. In 1948, the Fender company made a guitar with a completely solid body, which relied on electric amplification to make its sound. Since then, they have been made in all kinds of shapes.

Electric guitars are designed to produce special effects. Fender's early instruments had a "tremolo arm," a lever that could be used to alter the pitch of notes as they were being played. By adding electronic "effects units," often operated by foot pedals, guitarists can control a variety of unusual sounds. "Fuzz boxes" alter the notes to make them harsh and distorted, "delay" units add an echo, and "chorus" units make one guitar sound like many.

If you are a guitarist and you want to operate a synthesizer, you can now play the guitar synthesizer. It looks like a guitar, but its electronic "strings" operate a computer that can produce a full range of electronic sounds.

A classical electric guitar, showing its completely solid body

The lead, seen here, carries the electric signals from this bass guitar to the amplifier. Unlike the ordinary electric guitar, the bass guitar has only four thick strings.

THE BASS GUITAR

There have been attempts to build large acoustic guitars with a lower range than the ordinary instrument, but none were really successful. Leo Fender invented the modern **bass** guitar in 1951. It is about the same size as an ordinary guitar and has four thick strings tuned to the same notes as a double bass. In many kinds of rock music the bass guitar repeats patterns of low notes beneath the other instruments.

THE BANJO

The banjo, which has four, five, and sometimes six strings, is used in jazz, blues, folk, and country music. It was developed in the United States in the 1800s, and has a long guitarlike neck and a round body. This consists of a metal hoop and a tight vellum or nylon skin stretched over it, somewhat like a drum. The banjo is plucked or strummed with a plectrum, and its metal strings and vellum soundboard give it a strident, ringing sound.

Guitar Playing

The guitar is a very popular instrument, but although many people start to learn, a large number give up soon afterward. It is not as easy to play as it looks. Choose the type of guitar that suits the kind of music you want to play. To play the classical guitar, you'll need to learn to read music and play a Spanish guitar with nylon strings. For rock music, you'll need an electric guitar, and you'll need to learn to read a special way of writing out harmony called "chord symbols."

Listening Guide

There are many records of classical guitar solos, made by the great players of the century, such as Andre Segovia, Julian Bream, and John Williams. Special concertos were written for the guitar by Rodriguez and Villa-Lobos.

One of the most remarkable jazz guitarists is Stanley Jordan, who can play separate melodies with each hand, giving the effect of two guitarists at once!

Stanley Jordan

The Lute

Lute Playing

Very few people start to play the lute without first having learned the guitar. Reading lute music (which is written as a kind of fingering chart called "tablature") is very hard. Instruments are expensive and quite rare. The lute was a popular instrument for minstrels in the Middle Ages.

In the Middle Ages, and right up to the start of the 18th century, one of the most widely used string instruments was the lute. The lute has a "vaulted" body, made from strips of wood, or "ribs," glued together into roughly the shape of a pear. At the front is a flat soundboard. Many lutes have a rose-shaped sound hole with elaborate and beautiful patterns carved into it. The strings are joined to the bridge and run from there to the pegbox across a broad fingerboard with gut frets.

The lute has its pegbox set at a sharp angle, and up to 13 courses of strings are common. If each course consists of two strings, this means many lutes have 26 strings. As makers built lutes with more and more strings, they added them at the lower end of the instrument's **compass** (or range). The lower strings are tuned to play the notes of a descending scale, from the highest note to the lowest. This means that the lute player can choose the right bass notes without having to use left-hand fingering.

The lute came from the Middle East and was probably brought to Europe by people returning from the Crusades.

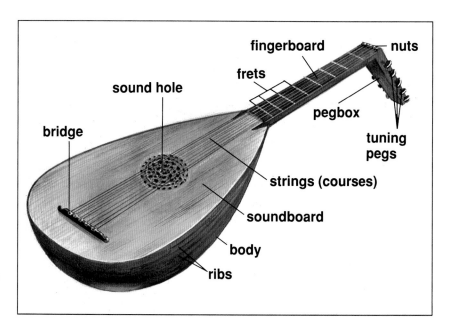

LARGE LUTES

When the lute was used to accompany singers, the bass notes of the lower strings and the stopped chords of the upper strings produced such a pleasant effect that builders started to make these lutes with very long extensions to their necks. These carried extra **unstopped** bass strings. The archlute, the *chitarrone*, and the *theorbo* are all examples of these extended lutes. Most of them have a second pegbox at the extreme end of the neck for the bass strings.

Julian Bream

RELATED INSTRUMENTS

Between 1200 and 1350, the *citole* was a popular instrument. It was a close relation to the medieval fiddle, but it was held and played more like a lute, except that a plectrum (made of bone) or a quill was used to pluck the strings. *Citoles* were made from one piece of wood, skillfully carved to form the pegbox, neck, and body, although the soundboard was glued on afterward.

The *cittern* and its close cousin the *cithrinchen* were also generally made from a single piece of wood. These instruments were played with a plectrum and had wire strings. They were very popular in the 16th century. Like lutes, they usually had a beautifully carved "rose" sound hole.

The mandolin has been made in styles similar to the *cittern* (from one piece of wood) and the lute (with a swell-back built of ribs). Today it is still a popular folk instrument. It has a lute-shaped sound box, a short fingerboard, and a pegbox like that of a guitar.

There are many relations of the lute family in use around the world. The "*Ud*" is an Arabic instrument that is the ancestor of the modern lute. The long-necked *tânbur* from the Middle East, the *tambura*, *sita*, and *vina*, all from India and Pakistan, are other common varieties.

This theorbo, made in Venice in 1638, is an example of the extended lute. You can see the second pegbox at the end of the neck.

The Harp

The modern concert harp is a relatively young member of one of the most ancient musical families. In its present form it dates from 1810, but its ancestors go back over 4,000 years.

All harps have a sound box or resonator to which the strings are attached on one end, and a neck to which they are attached at the other—either directly or through tuning pegs or keys. The modern harp, like many of its forebears, also has a "column" that runs parallel to the longest string, joining the sound box and the neck.

Each string on the harp is plucked to produce a different note. As there are 47 strings, some are colored to help players find their way about the instrument. The pedals operate a system of levers that change the notes played by each string. This gives the harp a very wide range.

Harps have been shown in sculpture and paintings from the time of the ancient Egyptians to the present. One very famous picture shows the biblical King David playing the harp. If we compare the harps shown by artists over the centuries we can learn about the instruments used in different countries at different times. One well-known variety is the Irish harp, or *cláirseach*, a relatively small instrument with between 24 and 34 strings. This is often used by students starting to learn the harp, before they begin to play the bigger concert instrument. One of the oldest Irish harps, known as the "Brian Boru" harp, is preserved in Trinity College in Dublin.

The basic design of the modern double action harp (shown above) has changed very little from the harp played in this wall painting, found in an Egyptian rock tomb dating from around 1500 B.C.

Harp Playing

The harp is a big and unwieldy instrument. Not many people learn to play it, partly because it takes up a lot of space and is difficult to move. To start learning you need to be big enough to reach the strings easily and to operate the pedals.

Harp Music

Many composers have written music for the harp, both as a solo instrument and as part of the orchestra. It has been used in many small chamber groups where its range and delicate sound make it ideal. Watch for recordings by Marisa Robles. The Welsh **virtuoso** Osian Ellis is also a leading player of *penillion*, in which a harpist plays a well-known tune and at the same time sings a new melody with Welsh words.

Jane Lister playing a concert harp

THE ZITHER

The modern zither comes from south Germany and Austria and consists of a somewhat flat sound box with two sets of strings set across it. One group (usually with five strings) has a fretboard, like a guitar's, and the player stops these with the left hand, plucking notes with a plectrum held on the right thumb. The second group consists of "open" strings, plucked by the remaining fingers of the player's right hand.

The Hawaiian guitar looks like a cross between a guitar and a zither. It is played flat across the knees (or on a separate tripod), and players slide a steel bar along the strings to change the notes in the familiar swooping **glissandos** of Hawaiian music.

An Austrian zither player

♩ Glossary

accompany   support other players and instruments by playing with them

acoustic guitar   the traditional guitar with no amplification

alto   lower range of notes sung by a female voice

bass   lowest range of notes sung by an adult male voice

bridge   movable piece of wood over which strings (of a violin, etc.) are stretched

chamber music   music played in a small concert room, by a small group of musicians

chord   group of notes sounded together

compass   range of a voice

consort   group of several players performing together

extension   additional part (of the instrument)

fingerboard   the section of a string instrument on which the fingers of the left hand alter the vibrating length of the strings

fingering   using the fingers to play a passage in a particular way

finger picking   using the fingers to play a melody and pluck chords at the same time

fret   bar or ridge on fingerboard that determines the finger positions to produce the required notes

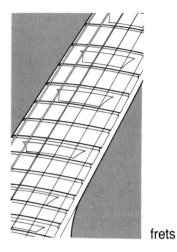

frets

frog   the adjustable block on a bow to which the hairs are attached

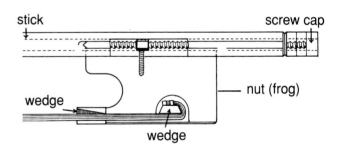

stick / screw cap / wedge / nut (frog) / wedge

glissando   music made by drawing finger or bow quickly up and down a series of adjacent notes

jazz   music of black American origin with characteristic harmony and syncopated rhythm, often improvised

key   the device used to adjust the tension of a string

machine heads   gears that adjust the tension of the strings

nut   the ridge at the upper end of the neck that keeps the strings from touching the fingerboard

octave   eight notes of a complete scale

pegbox   frame in which the tuning pegs are fitted

pickup   magnetic device that transmits sound as electrical signals to an amplifier

pitch   level of a note, indicated by its position on the scale

pizzicato   sound made by plucking the string

plectrum   triangle of horn, shell, or plastic used to pluck the strings

quartet   group of four performers; piece of music composed for four performers; usually the string quartet is two violins, a viola, and a cello

ragtime   music with a syncopated melody that is played against a regularly accented bass

resonate   to amplify a sound and make it louder or stronger

scroll   the carved end of a peg box

solo   a piece of music performed by one person

soprano   highest range of notes sung by a female voice

soundboard   the front or "belly" of a string instrument on which the bridge is set

sound box   the body of a stringed instrument

soundpost

stop(ping)   placing the tips of the fingers of the left hand so that they shorten the vibrating string

tenor   highest range of notes sung by an adult male voice

tension   the tightness of a string

tone   the type or quality of a sound

tuning   setting the strings of an instrument at a particular pitch

unstopped   an open string

virtuoso   someone especially skilled at playing a particular instrument

volume   loudness or softness of a sound

 Index